D1180767

weblinks

You don't need a computer to use this book. But, for readers who do have access to the Internet, the book provides links to recommended websites which offer additional information and resources on the subject.

You will find weblinks boxes like this on some pages of the book.

weblinks

For more information about Stella McCartney, go to www.waylinks.co.uk /21CentLives/Fashion

waylinks.co.uk

To help you find the recommended websites easily and quickly, weblinks are provided on our own website, **waylinks.co.uk**. These take you straight to the relevant websites and save you typing in the Internet address yourself.

Internet safety

↗ Never give out personal details, which include: your name, address, school, telephone number, email address, password and mobile number.

↗ Do not respond to messages which make you feel uncomfortable – tell an adult.

↗ Do not arrange to meet in person someone you have met on the Internet.

↗ Never send your picture or anything else to an online friend without a parent's or teacher's permission.

↗ If you see anything that worries you, tell an adult.

A *note to adults*
Internet use by children should be supervised. We recommend that you install filtering software which blocks unsuitable material.

Website content

The weblinks for this book are checked and updated regularly. However, because of the nature of the Internet, the content of a website may change at any time, or a website may close down without notice. While the Publishers regret any inconvenience this may cause readers, they cannot be responsible for the content of any website other than their own.

HODDER
Wayland

21st CENTURY LIVES
FASHION DESIGNERS

Liz Gogerly

HODDER
Wayland

an imprint of Hodder Children's Books

Editor: Hayley Leach
Design: Peter Bailey for Proof Books
Cover design: Hodder Children's Books

Published in Great Britain in 2004 by Hodder Wayland,
an imprint of Hodder Children's Books.

British Library Cataloguing in Publication Data
Gogerly, Liz
Fashion designers. – (21st Century lives)
1. Fashion designers – Biography – Juvenile literature
I. Title
746.9'2'0922

ISBN: 0750245964

Cover: Fashion designer Stella McCartney with supermodels Kirsty Hume and
Helena Christensen.

Picture acknowledgements: Cover Photo B.D.V./Corbis; 4 Beirne Brenda/Corbis Sygma;
5 Stephane Cardinale/People Avenue/Corbis; 6 Orban Thierry/Corbis Sygma;
7 Patrick Hertzog/AFP/Getty Images; 8 and 9 Stephane Cardinale/People
Avenue/Corbis; 10 Pace Gregory/Corbis Sygma; 11 PerreVerdy/AFP/Getty Images;
12 Steve Azzara/Corbis; 13 Petre Buzoianu/Corbis; Title page, 14 and15 Stephane
Cardinale/People Avenue/Corbis;16 Rune Hellestad/Corbis; 17 Jean-Pierre
Muller/AFP/Getty Images; 18 Gregory Pace/Corbis; 19 Gail Mooney/CORBIS;
20 Carlos Alvarez/Getty Images; 21 Jean-Pierre Muller/ AFP/Getty Images

Printed in China by WKT Company Ltd

Hodder Children's Books
a division of Hodder Headline Limited
338 Euston Road
London NW1 3BH

Contents

Stella McCartney

Stella McCartney is recognised for her bohemian style

" I design things I want but can't get. "

" I know what makes a chick tick. "
Stella McCartney

Name: Stella McCartney

Year and place of birth: 1971, London, UK

Education: Stella graduated from London's Central St Martin's College of Art and Design in 1995.

Fashion house: In 1997 Stella became Creative Director for the French fashion house Chloé. In 2001 she moved to the Italian house of Gucci to launch a new label under her own name.

Style: Bohemian and feminine, Stella takes her inspiration from the fashions of the past. To get a romantic effect she uses layers of delicate fabrics, lots of elaborate details and even some hand-painted designs. She mixes romantic, floaty tops and dresses with tailored trousers and suits.

Famous clients: Madonna, Kate Moss, Cameron Diaz and Nicole Kidman.

Something you might not know about her: She is passionate about animal rights. She once refused to work for Gucci because they used leather and fur in their designs. Now she works for Gucci but she produces designs under her own name and can choose what fabrics she wants to use.

Get the look! Don't be afraid to mix different styles and have fun with your clothes. Be funky and free, and team up your jeans with a pretty blouse you found in a charity shop. Sew beads, sequins, silk flowers or interesting buttons onto your clothes.

Stella McCartney is the daughter of the world-famous rock star and ex-Beatle Paul McCartney. Her mother Linda was a photographer and animal rights campaigner who established a vegetarian food company. As a little girl Stella was used to famous people visiting the family home in Sussex, England. But, in many other ways, her life was very normal and her parents sent her to a comprehensive school rather than paying for an expensive private education.

A love of clothes was in Stella's blood from an early age. She was inspired by the clothes she found in her mother's wardrobe and the old clothes she gathered at markets and charity shops. When she was 15 she worked with the top French designer Christian Lacroix. A few years later she studied fashion at Central St Martin's College of Art in London. Though other students teased her for being Paul McCartney's daughter Stella soon showed them that she had talent of her own.

Stella left college in 1995 then, in 1997, she joined the famous French fashion house, Chloé. At the age of just 25 she was appointed Chief Designer. Stella quickly established herself as one of the most exciting up and coming young designers. Her beautiful floaty dresses were popular with pop stars, models and actresses. Chloé's profits began to rise and so did Stella's reputation.

In 2001 Stella left Chloé to join the Gucci Group. At last she had the opportunity to launch a label under her own name. Though her new collections were greeted with mixed reviews Stella's clothes remain popular with women everywhere. Madonna chose Stella to design her wedding dress and the actress Kate Hudson wore one of Stella's gowns at the Oscars.

In 2002 and 2003 Stella opened her first shops in New York and London. Though still in her early-thirties Stella McCartney has already earned herself the reputation as one of the world's best designers.

A mixture of fabrics has been used to create this feminine design from McCartney's ready-to-wear collection 2003

"... if I could raid one person's closet it would be Stella McCartney's. I love her clothes. Can you imagine being able to borrow anything from her closet? Heaven!"

The American actress Kirsten Dunst

weblinks

For more information about Stella McCartney, go to
www.waylinks.co.uk/21CentLives/Fashion

Donatella Versace

Donatella Versace

> **"** Fashion is not frivolous...I am a businesswoman. I'm a very serious person. **"**
> **Donatella Versace**

Name: Donatella Versace

Year and place of birth: 1959, Reggio di Calabria, Southern Italy

Education: Donatella Versace studied language at Florence University, Italy but she left in 1979.

Fashion house: In 1993 she designed casual wear for Versace's label, Versus. In 1997, after the murder of her brother Gianni, she became Head of Design for the Versace group.

Style: Outrageous, extravagant and sexy. Donatella's clothes are created for women who aren't afraid to show off their wealth or their bodies. Donatella has taken the colourful, dramatic style made famous by her brother Gianni and added her own rock chick and feminine twist.

Famous clients: Jennifer Lopez, Elizabeth Hurley, Robbie Williams and Camilla Parker-Bowles.

Something you might not know about her: She loves jewellery. You won't catch Donatella without the giant diamond ring given to her by her brother. It's also said that she won't leave home unless she is wearing £100,000 worth of jewellery.

Get the look! Versace actually has different labels to suit many kinds of people. You'll find classic, young, funky and casual wear in the range. To get the classic Versace look you have to think hot summer nights and parties. Be bold and wear colourful clothes – even if they clash. Girls, add headscarves, jewellery and belts with tassels. Boys, don't forget your sunglasses.

Clothes and creativity have always been part of Donatella Versace's life. Her mother Francesca ran her own dressmaking shop and her brother Gianni founded Versace, one of the most successful fashion houses in modern times. When Donatella was a student in Florence she spent many of her weekends in Milan helping Gianni with fashion shoots and sometimes being his model. With her hair dyed platinum blonde and her love of contemporary music and fashion, Donatella had her own unique style. When Gianni was unsure about one of his creations he would often ask for Donatella's opinion.

In 1979 Donatella left college to take charge of PR (public relations) at Versace. During the 1980s she brought the label into the spotlight. Versace fashion shows always had the top models and the most sought after celebrities in the front row. Meanwhile, behind the scenes, Donatella was learning how to become a fashion designer from her brother. By the 1990s she was designing casual clothes for a brand new line within the Versace group, called Versus.

Gianni Versace was shot dead outside his home in Miami, USA in 1997. Donatella had lost her brother and best friend. She was in shock and immediately cancelled the next collection of clothes. It looked as if the great Versace fashion house was about to crumble. Fortunately, Donatella changed her mind and decided that her brother would have wanted her to head his fashion empire.

Many people questioned Donatella's ability to design but since 1998 the company has gone from strength to strength. Today Donatella is head of a top fashion house and is one of the most powerful businesswomen in Europe. At work, she is tough and she expects high standards from all her staff. At play, she is glitzy and glamorous and a celebrity party wouldn't be the same without her.

A colourful creation for the summer from Versace's Spring/Summer 2004 collection

"Donatella is a different voice. Although she is a more extrovert character than Gianni, her work is softer, a more modern femininity. While Gianni was great with big sculptural — almost statuesque — pieces that were in keeping with bold times, she goes for a more organic pattern making what seems right today."

Claire Wilcox, curator of the 2002 exhibition of Versace at the Victoria & Albert Museum in London

weblinks

For more information about Donatella Versace, go to
www.waylinks.co.uk/21CentLives/Fashion

Vivienne Westwood

Vivienne Westwood

> " Life is an adventure, so I make clothes to have adventures in... They give you power over rich people, because you can look more chic than they ever can. "
> Vivienne Westwood

Vivienne Westwood: An Unfashionable Life
by Jane Mulvagh
(Harper Collins, 1999)

Name: Vivienne Westwood

Year and place of birth: 1941, Glossop, Derbyshire, UK

Education: Vivienne graduated from teacher training college in the 1960s.

Fashion house: In 1981 Vivienne showed her first collection of women's clothing in London. In the following years she established her own label. In 1990 she added menswear to her collection. In recent times she has launched her own perfume, make-up and eyewear.

Style: Daring English eccentric. Vivienne takes inspiration from history. Many of her clothes are re-workings of period costumes. She has used everything, from Elizabethan to twentieth century styles. She updates the look by exaggerating the original style. She might shorten the hemline, tighten the corset or use exciting new fabrics.

Something you might not know about her: Vivienne is the original punk queen. In 1971 she cut off her long hair, dyed it peroxide-blonde and spiked it up. This style became popular in the late 1970s when punk became fashionable. She was also responsible for dressing the punk band the Sex Pistols.

Get the look! Why not try to recreate Vivienne's punk fashions from the 1970s. To get this look you have to experiment with new ideas of your own. As a starting point you could take old clothes you no longer wear and give them new life by ripping them then adding zips, badges and safety pins. You can pick-up ordinary t-shirts from charity shops and re-vamp them by tearing off the sleeves, cutting the shoulder seams, then knotting them back together.

In 1992 Vivienne Westwood was at Buckingham Palace collecting an OBE (Officer of the Order of the British Empire) from the Queen for services to British fashion. Nearly two decades before this Vivienne had been designing the kind of rebellious clothes that people of the Queen's generation found shocking.

Vivienne Westwood's colourful life began in 1941, far away from London, in Glossop, Derbyshire. In 1957 she moved to Harrow in London and by 1963 she was married and had started a family. She worked as a typist before becoming a teacher. By 1965 she had begun to feel that her life was rather boring. She left her husband, met a young man called Malcolm Edwards (later known as Malcolm McLaren) and moved to South London.

In London Vivienne and Malcolm opened a boutique on the King's Road. They sold daring, fashionable clothes for young people. By 1974 the shop was selling Vivienne's ripped t-shirts and other items of punk clothing that she made. Then, in 1976 the punk band the Sex Pistols burst onto the music scene. Malcolm was their manager and the band was dressed in Vivienne's clothes.

Vivienne led the way in punk fashion. Then, in 1981, she showed there was more to her than rips and safety pins. She put together a collection of clothes themed around pirates. Her dashing and original designs were popular and in 1983 she took her collection to Paris. In the following years Vivienne's reputation as an exciting and imaginative designer grew. In 1990 and 1991 she won the award for British Fashion Designer of the Year.

Today, Vivienne has stores in New York, Paris, London and the Far East. Even though she is successful she lives a simple life: "All I've got at home are two second-hand armchairs, a trestle table, a fridge and a cooker." She also likes cycling to work.

Models take to the catwalk in creations from Vivienne Westwood's Autumn/Winter 2003/04 collection

"It is a lesson in life that anyone, from any walk of life, in any sphere can take. That despite class, club, the right financial connections, if you have the commitment and desire to succeed, you can. That is Vivienne's story. In the face of monumental adversity, she sat down at the machine and sewed a shirt. That's a fairy tale."

The designer Jeff Banks on Vivienne Westwood
Vivienne Westwood: An Unfashionable Life by Jane Mulvagh (Harper Collins, 1999)

weblinks

For more information about Vivienne Westwood, go to
www.waylinks.co.uk/21CentLives/Fashion

Helmut Lang

Helmut Lang at the Vogue *Fashion Awards*

Name: Helmut Lang

Year and place of birth: 1956, Vienna, Austria

Education: Helmut studied at business school in Austria.

Fashion house: Helmut started his own fashion studio in 1977. In the mid-1980s he opened his first shop in Vienna. He relocated his business to New York in 1998. In 1999 he sold part of his business to the Prada fashion house.

Style: Ultra-modern, cool and casual. Helmut's clothes come in a range of neutral colours — you'll find lots of black, grey, white, brown and beige in his collections. He favours razor-sharp straight lines — men's trousers are often close-fitting and women's clothes are plain but well-cut. Many of his outfits look like something from the future.

Famous clients: David Beckham, Natalie Portman and Uma Thurman.

Something you might not know about him: He's a regular subscriber to the *National Geographic* magazine. He also became the first fashion designer to advertise in the magazine.

Get the look! Think urban and cool. Don't reach for any bright colours and always choose matching colours. If in doubt go for black, black and more black. Hunt for simple clothes in high-tech fabrics. Suits should be sharp, and shirts should be crisp. Add polish to your look by slicking back your hair.

The king of urban chic was born in Vienna, Austria in 1956. Like so many of his famous clothes there is something cool and mysterious about Helmut Lang. He keeps his personal life private and he doesn't do many interviews.

Helmut started working in the fashion world when he had difficulty finding the kind of clothes that he wanted to wear. He studied at business school and looked set to become a businessman but he soon discovered he couldn't find the jackets or t-shirts that he liked so he switched to a career in fashion. In 1977 he opened a studio in Vienna and by the middle of the 1980s his ready-to-wear collections were big news in Austria. His clothes were cutting edge and modern. He experimented with unusual high-tech fabrics. His look worked well for the smart young go-getters of the 1980s.

In 1986 Helmut was so popular at home that he was invited by the Austrian government to exhibit his clothes in a national exhibition in France. It was the first time that Helmut had shown his clothes outside his own country and they were a hit. Paris is the centre of the fashion industry in Europe but Helmut remained in Vienna. It was many years before he was tempted to move and when he did he relocated to New York, USA in the late 1990s.

Helmut Lang now has boutiques in New York, Vienna, Munich in Germany, and Milan in Italy. He has ranges of aftershave, perfume, eyewear, shoes and underwear. In 1997 he added jeans to his line. However, his ready-to-wear collections for men and women remain his best selling items. In 1999 he sold a large share of his company to the fashion giant Prada. What will happen next is as much a mystery as the man himself.

A model wears a jacket that looks as if it has come straight out of the future from Lang's ready-to-wear Spring/Summer 2004 collection

"Lang's watchwords are 'now', 'urban', 'clean' and 'modern'. His clothes reflect an effortless, downbeat style which is instantly recognisable."

The Fashion Book edited by Richard Martin
(Phaidon Press Ltd, 1998)

weblinks

For more information about Helmut Lang, go to
www.waylinks.co.uk/21CentLives/Fashion

Donna Karan

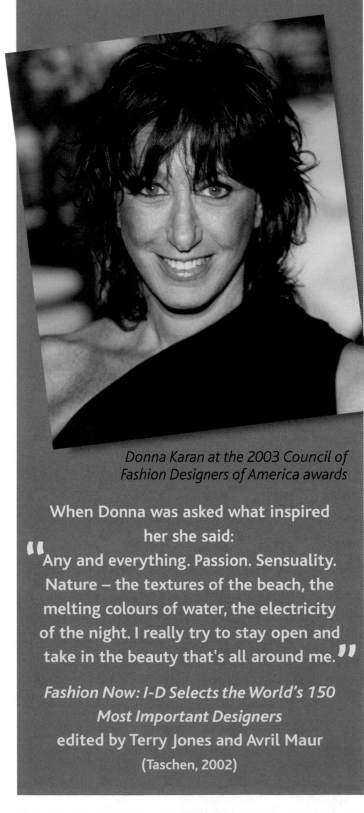

Donna Karan at the 2003 Council of Fashion Designers of America awards

When Donna was asked what inspired her she said:

"Any and everything. Passion. Sensuality. Nature – the textures of the beach, the melting colours of water, the electricity of the night. I really try to stay open and take in the beauty that's all around me."

Fashion Now: I-D Selects the World's 150 Most Important Designers
edited by Terry Jones and Avril Maur
(Taschen, 2002)

Name: Donna Karan

Year and place of birth: 1948, Forest Hills, New York, USA

Education: Donna worked for the designer Liz Claiborne during her school summer holidays. She attended Parsons School of Design, New York in the mid-1960s.

Fashion house: In 1967 Donna went straight from college to work for Anne Klein & Co. In 1985 she showed her first Donna Karan collection; then in 1988 she launched the famous DKNY (Donna Karan New York) label.

Style: Modern, affordable and stylish. Donna designs clothes for successful young people who want to look good without trying too hard. Over the years she has experimented with many different styles – anything from business clothes to new age jeans and t-shirts. She makes good quality, wearable clothes for the daytime but her eveningwear can be floaty and flamboyant.

Famous clients: Cate Blanchett, Jennifer Aniston and Bruce Willis.

Something you might not know about her: Donna is so obsessed by the colour black that nearly everything in her New York apartment is black. Her daughter Gabby claims that when she was a baby her mother mainly dressed her in black too.

Get the look! Donna's early collections were based around a few key pieces of clothing. These clothes could be mixed and matched so that a person had something to wear everyday for any occasion. To get this look try to buy simple clothes in the same colour or in matching tones. These key pieces can be smartened up by adding a tailored jacket, or turned into eveningwear by slipping on a pretty sequin top or a fitted t-shirt.

One of the most famous names in American fashion and the woman behind the DKNY empire is a native New Yorker. Donna Karan was born in 1948 and lived in Long Island. Her step-father was a tailor and her mother was a model. As a girl Donna's hobbies were fashion and making clothes. After school she went straight to college, then into a job with the designer Anne Klein. Quickly rising through the ranks, Donna became Associate Designer before heading the design team when Anne Klein died in 1974.

It seemed like Donna had already made it in the fashion world, but in 1984 she took the plunge and launched her own label. Donna's collection soon caught the eye of women with busy lives. Her clothes looked good, were comfortable to wear, could be worn for any occasion and they didn't cost too much. It was a winning combination that brought Donna to the forefront of American fashion. In 1988 she added to her collection by launching the cheaper DKNY range. This line was inspired by her teenage daughter and had a more casual and everyday feel to it.

By the 1990s it seemed like the DKNY logo was everywhere. Donna introduced menswear, DKNY Jeans, DKNY Kids, City DKNY and DKNY fragrances. She also opened a string of shops and outlets throughout the world.

Donna is a sharp businesswoman but she's also a free spirit who's interested in meditation and Eastern philosophy. In 2001 her husband and business partner died. In the same year she announced that she had sold her business to a French company but she was still in charge of the creative process.

These days Donna can concentrate on her designs. In 2003 her new collection was proof that she hadn't lost her touch. Her models paraded down the catwalk in New York wearing skin-tight catsuits and slinky dresses. The fashion press were delighted.

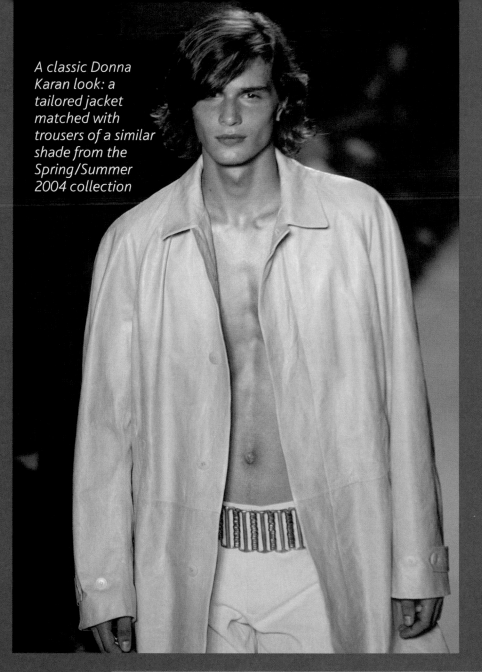

A classic Donna Karan look: a tailored jacket matched with trousers of a similar shade from the Spring/Summer 2004 collection

"Donna Karan...was on top form. She gave us the smooth tailoring and soft draping we expect from her.... She is one of American fashion's great talents, and rarely misses a beat"

The Sunday Times, 22 February 2004, after New York Fashion Week 2004

weblinks

For more information about Donna Karan, go to
www.waylinks.co.uk/21CentLives/Fashion

John Galliano

John Galliano at his
Spring/Summer 2004 collection

"More and more, we need to take in London. We visit London six to eight times per year, to get its spirit. We use the streets, the clubs, the libraries... we always go to the markets – Camden, Portobello – and the V&A [Victoria and Albert Museum]."
John Galliano, 1997

Galliano by Colin McDowell
(Cassell, 1997)

Name: John Galliano

Year and place of birth: 1960, Gibraltar

Education: John graduated from London's Central St Martin's College of Art and Design with a first-class degree in 1984.

Fashion house: He launched his own label in London in 1984 and moved to Paris in 1995 where he became Designer-in-Chief for the house of Givenchy. In 1996 he became the top designer at Christian Dior, possibly the most famous fashion house of all time.

Style: Galliano raids history books and film archives to produce some of the most outrageous and ambitious clothes that you'll ever find on a catwalk. Each year his collection is inspired by something different. In the past he has been influenced by 1930s Berlin and Bollywood movies (Indian films). In 2003 he whisked back to the 1940s for a touch of Hollywood movie glamour.

Famous clients: Kate Moss, Nicole Kidman and Madonna.

Something you might not know about him: He is a fitness fanatic. He gets up at 6am each morning so that he can work out with a fitness instructor for 40 minutes. Afterwards, he takes a six-mile run. During his jog through Paris he claims he has time to look around and find ideas for his next collection.

Get the look! Be prepared to take a flight of fancy and dress up like you've never done before. Whichever era Galliano is trying to capture his look is mostly romantic with plenty of ruffles and bows. If you decide to go Bollywood or Hollywood then keep your clothes flowing but show off your best features. Don't be scared of vibrant colours and remember to pay attention to your accessories too.

When John Galliano was chosen by Givenchy to be their Chief Designer he became the first British designer to head a French fashion house. During his short stay with Givenchy he created some of the most shocking and sensational clothes ever produced by the label.

John was born far away from the fashion world, in Gibraltar, to a Spanish mother and English father. When he was six the family moved to London, England. He did well at school and scooped a first class degree at Central St Martin's School of Art and Design in London in 1983. For his degree show he produced a striking collection influenced by the French Revolution. It was a massive hit and many of his clothes were bought by top boutiques in London and Paris.

Spurred on by his success John launched his own label in 1984. Famed for his romantic dresses and his beautifully tailored suits, John soon established himself as one of the most original and talented young designers of his generation. In 1987 he was voted British Fashion Designer of the Year.

In the fashion world talent doesn't always guarantee success. In London John struggled to raise the finance to produce his collections. In 1991 he moved to Paris but lack of money still made it difficult to survive. His luck seemed to change in1995 when he was hired by Givenchy. Unfortunately, his clothes were too wild for the traditional fashion house, and he left after just two collections.

Now John is head of design for Christian Dior. His clothes are as exciting and exotic as ever and are worn by some of the world's most glamorous women. Madonna and Nicole Kidman have appeared in his beautiful Dior creations for major events such as the Oscars. John's next venture is to open a boutique in Paris. He claims that he will host dinner parties in the shop window.

One of Galliano's outrageous designs – you wouldn't normally see this on the high street!

weblinks

For more information about
John Galliano, go to
www.waylinks.co.uk/21CentLives/Fashion

"John is from the school of perfection where the stitching in the lining must be as perfect as the stitches that can be seen."

The shoe designer Manolo Blahnik
Galliano by Colin McDowell (Cassell, 1997)

15

Paul Smith

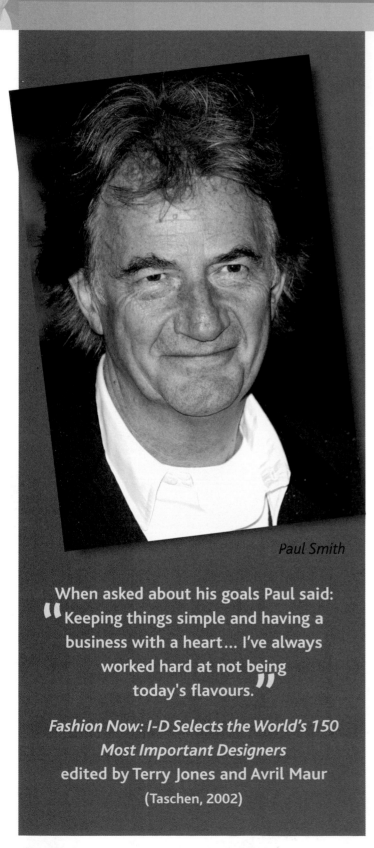

Paul Smith

When asked about his goals Paul said:
"Keeping things simple and having a business with a heart... I've always worked hard at not being today's flavours."

Fashion Now: I-D Selects the World's 150 Most Important Designers
edited by Terry Jones and Avril Maur
(Taschen, 2002)

Name: Paul Smith

Year and place of birth: 1947, Nottingham, England

Education: He left school at 15 with no qualifications. Later, he took evening classes in tailoring.

Fashion house: Paul opened his first boutique in Nottingham in 1970 and took his first Paul Smith collection to Paris in 1976. Today there are about 225 Paul Smith shops or outlets around the world. His collections include Paul Smith, Paul Smith Women, Paul Smith London, Paul Smith Shoes, Paul Smith Fragrances, Paul Smith Watches and Paul Smith Furniture.

Style: Paul sums up his own style as combining craftsmanship and tradition with a sense of humour. In past collections Paul re-invented fashions from the 1940s through to the 1970s. In 2003 he took inspiration from the punk fashions of the 1970s. His up-dated version did away with rips and safety pins and in its place was something softer and more modern.

Famous clients: The England Football team. Paul designed shoes, watches, luggage and cufflinks for the players to take to Japan for the 2002 World Cup.

Something you might not know about him: In 2000 Paul was knighted for his services to British fashion. So, he is now Sir Paul Smith.

Get the look! Think yesteryear with a twist. Men, you can inject life into a traditional grey suit by teaming it with a flowery shirt. Add a pair of unusual cufflinks from a charity shop and you've got the look. Women, you can buy well-made, tailored clothes in high street shops, then give them your personal stamp by changing the buttons. The finishing touch would be a beautiful old scarf you found in your grandma's wardrobe.

Traditional suits with bright shirts and accessories from Paul Smith's ready-to-wear collection Autumn/Winter 2004/05

Paul Smith's life is a true rags to riches tale. It began when he left school at 15. His father sold fabric door-to-door so Paul followed his footsteps into the rag trade. Paul's first job was in a clothing warehouse but he was more interested in his cycle ride to work than in his job. His boyhood dream of becoming a professional bicycle racer was dashed when he was involved in a bike crash. Around this time he became friendly with some students from the local art college. He was inspired by their ideas and realized he wanted to do something creative for a living.

Paul's girlfriend Pauline Denyer had studied fashion design and she encouraged him to study design at night school and to open a male boutique. He opened his first shop in Nottingham in 1970. The clothes were mostly his own designs but behind the scenes he was going through a crash course in pattern making and tailoring. Even in these early days Paul's designs were unusual but they did not catch on immediately. For a few years he did other jobs to survive and he considered fashion to be almost a hobby rather than a proper career.

Fortunately, Paul did not waver and continued to produce the kind of men's clothes that he liked. He chose unusual fabrics and added clever details to the clothes. His first collection in Paris in 1976 established him as a bright new talent. A few years later he opened a shop in London. His hands-on approach to his business and the fact that he continued to work in his shop meant he could keep an eye on changing trends. When he noticed that women came into the shop to buy his men's suits for themselves he launched a women's label too.

These days Paul has shops in Nottingham, London, Paris, Milan, New York and Hong Kong. He's most popular in Japan where he has opened 200 shops. Despite his fame and his fortune he is one of the most down-to-earth and modest designers in the fashion business.

"His designs are famous for being classic with a twist. Elegant yet surprising combinations of textiles and meticulous craftsmanship are his trademarks. His clothes are upmarket to say the least and are the garb [clothing] of casual jet setters and the international celebrities."

Rome Jorge, journalist for the *Manila Times*, August, 2003

weblinks

For more information about Paul Smith, go to
www.waylinks.co.uk/21CentLives/Fashion

Manolo Blahnik

Manolo Blahnik with one of his biggest fans, Sarah Jessica Parker

" My shows don't change drastically from season to season...I think it's awfully rude to ask someone to pay a lot of money for a pair of shoes, and then have them be 'out' the next season. People are not stupid. They know what they want, and they should get it. "
Manolo Blahnik

Name: Manolo Blahnik

Year and place of birth: 1943, Canary Islands, Spain

Education: Manolo studied architecture and literature at the University of Geneva but he left before getting a qualification. Later he studied traditional shoemaking in East London and Northampton, England. The Royal College of Art and the Royal Society of Arts of Britain awarded him with honourary doctorates.

Fashion house: He began designing shoes in 1971 and opened his first shop selling his own designs in London in 1973. Later he opened a shop in New York.

Style: More talked about than walked on, Manolo's shoes are like miniature works of art. He uses fur and feathers, diamanté and sequins, embroidery and fancy stitching to turn his shoes into little show pieces. Also, expect to see very high heels – sometimes they are over 12cm tall!

Famous clients: Madonna, Kylie Minogue, Princesss Diana and Marge Simpson from *The Simpsons*.

Something you might not know about him: In 2002 Manolo had to take a pair of his shoes off the market because they were too dangerous. The shoes in question had metal heels that were nearly 8cm high and just 3mm wide. They were so sharp they could cut through carpet. On the wrong feet they could be used as a weapon!

Get the look! Take inspiration from the ballet and the theatre. You can change a pair of old shoes you no longer wear into something new and exciting by gluing ribbon, artificial flowers, buttons or pieces of material onto them. Think of Cinderella and add gold or silver objects to a pair of boring sandals. Soon, you'll have something that looks like it stepped out of a fairytale.

The most famous shoe designer of the twenty-first century picked his career by accident. His extraordinary life began on the Canary Islands in Spain. Raised by his Spanish mother and Czech father, he grew up miles away from the fashion capitals of Europe – his early years were spent on a banana plantation. Later, he began a degree in architecture and literature at the University of Geneva in Switzerland but in 1968 he left to live in Paris before he qualified. A few years later he moved to London.

Manolo took a job as a photographer with *The Sunday Times* newspaper. He started mixing with actors, models and other fashionable people. In his spare time he was sketching ideas for stage sets and shoes. By chance one of his friends introduced him to the Editor of American *Vogue*, fashion magazine. When he showed her his sketches she told him to forget stage work and make shoes.

In 1971 Manolo started working with the up and coming British designer Ossie Clark. Ossie was famous for his outrageous clothes but Manolo was not to be outdone. Among his creations was a pair of green suede shoes with fake cherries. The heels were so high the models hobbled down the catwalk. These funky new shoes caught the eye of famous models and actresses. Soon afterwards Manolo perfected his art by attending classes in shoemaking. Then, in 1973 he opened a tiny shop in London called Zapata. He designed each shoe and crafted the original shoe from which each design was then copied.

Today, Manolo has shops in London and New York and four factories in Italy. Famous popstars, actresses and models all want to wear his creations. 'Manolo' has become another word for stylish shoes. Despite his success Manolo is still closely involved in the production of each design. He sketches the design, selects the fabrics and materials and keeps a keen eye on production in Italy. Now he's in his sixties but he shows no sign of slowing down.

A velvet pump by Manolo: notice the quilted detail inside the shoe

"You can take my Fendi baguette [bag], you can take my ring and my watch, but don't take my Manolo Blahniks."

Sarah Jessica Parker's character, Carrie Bradshaw, from the popular television series *Sex and the City*

weblinks

For more information about Manolo Blahnik, go to
www.waylinks.co.uk/21CentLives/Fashion

Alexander McQueen at the Marie Clare Fashion Awards 2003

When asked about the drive behind his work Alexander said:

" To make a piece that can transcend any trend and will still hold as much presence in 100 years time when you find it in an antique store as when you bought it in my store yesterday. "

Fashion Now: I-D Selects the World's 150 Most Important Designers
edited by Terry Jones and Avril Maur
(Taschen, 2002)

Name: Alexander McQueen (He changed his name from Lee to Alexander when he launched his fashion career.)

Year and place of birth: 1969, London

Education: Alexander left school at 16 to become an apprentice for a tailor on Savile Row in London. He graduated from London's Central St Martins College of Art and Design in 1993 with a degree in fashion design.

Fashion house: As a teenager, Alexander worked for the Japanese designer Koji Tatsuno and Romeo Gigli in Milan, Italy. In 1993 he set up his own label but in 1996 he became Head of Design for Givenchy in Paris. In 2001 he returned to London to relaunch his own label.

Style: Dramatic, theatrical and totally unpredictable. Alexander isn't scared to borrow ideas from everywhere and anywhere. In the past his collections have been inspired by Spanish flamenco dancers, cowgirls and Native Americans. Even though his clothes can be wild and outrageous, he is recognized as one of the best tailors in the business.

Famous clients: Kate Winslet, David Bowie, Madonna and Whitney Houston.

Something you might not know about him: The British actress Kate Winslet turns to Alexander when she needs a dress for a special occasion. For the 1998 Oscars she wore a romantic green dress designed by Alexander. When she married later that year he made her wedding dress.

Get the look! Use your imagination and be adventurous. Enjoy mixing colours and different styles together so you have a look that is absolutely individual to you. In 2003 Alexander showed a jacket made from white pom-poms which looked like snowballs. In the past he's created clothes from jigsaw puzzles.

McQueen uses his imagination
in this creation from his
Autumn/Winter 2003/04
ready-to-wear collection

Alexander McQueen was born in the East End of London and his father was a taxi driver. He has tattoos and a shaved head. For many years he was known as the 'bad boy' of fashion. These days he is one of the most important fashion designers in the world.

Alexander went to an all-boys schools but he soon realized he was a bit different to the other children. He dreamed of going to art college and spent his time sketching women's clothes. Eventually he left school at 16 but his dreams of art college didn't come true until his early twenties. By this time he'd learned how to cut fabric as a tailor in Savile Row. He had worked for a theatrical tailor and acquired his taste for dramatic clothes. He'd also worked for top fashion designers and lived and worked in Italy.

In 1993 Alexander graduated from Central St Martins College of Art and Design. His degree show got rave reviews from the fashion press. Encouraged by their praise, Alexander set up his own label in London. In the following years his wild designs caused quite a stir. One of his most famous creations were the 'bumster' trousers, which were a bit like hipster jeans but went even lower. Many people said his clothes were not practical and couldn't be worn. Even so, Alexander picked up many admirers, particularly models and popstars. In 1996 and 1997 he won the award for British Fashion Designer of the Year.

In 1997 Alexander became Chief Designer for the famous French house of Givenchy. It was a great honour but he was unhappy there because he felt he wasn't allowed to be creative. In 2001 he was delighted to be back in London with his own label. Now his collections are as bold and exciting as ever. Each show is like a night at the theatre. Whatever he does brings sparkle and fun to the fashion industry.

"I love Alexander McQueen. He's really creative. He's always ready to surprise. From season to season, you never really know what to expect, but it always works."

The British model, Sophie Dahl

weblinks

For more information about
Alexander McQueen, go to
www.waylinks.co.uk/21CentLives/Fashion

Other Fashion Designers

Jean-Paul Gaultier

Known as the 'bad boy' of French fashion, Jean-Paul Gaultier was born in Paris in 1952. Fashion obsessed him from an early age and his first jobs were with the houses of Pierre Cardin and Jacques Esterel. He showed his first collection in 1978 and went on to become one of the most exciting young designers of the 1980s.

Jean-Paul's fashions have always caused excitement. In his time he has created dresses for men and brought back the basque (tight-fitting bodice) for women. In 1990 he was commissioned by the singer Madonna to design her costumes for the Blonde Ambition tour. The pointed basque she wore became one of the most talked about costumes for years. Jean-Paul also designs for the ballet and for film. In 1997 he made the costumes for the film *The Fifth Element*. In 2003 he became chief designer for the House of Hermés, in Paris.

Issey Miyake

The Japanese designer Issey Miyake was born in Hiroshima, in 1935. He studied graphic design at Tama Art University in Tokyo before moving to Paris. In the French capital he worked for the designer Guy Laroche before moving to the fashion house of Givenchy. In the early 1970s he moved to New York to work for the designer Geoffrey Beene. By 1971 he was back in Tokyo and opened his first studio. In the same year he launched his first collection in New York and by 1973 his designs were seen on the Paris catwalks. He formed his own label in France in 1979 and in the USA in 1989.

Many of his clothes are so beautifully made or innovative that they are like museum pieces. He combines eastern and western influences to create a striking avant-garde look. Though his clothes are often in muted colours they are still dramatic. He manages to achieve this by using a mixture of different fabrics and cutting or pleating the garments in unusual ways.

Vera Wang

The American designer Vera Wang has built a reputation on her beautiful wedding dresses and evening gowns. She was born in 1949 in New York, USA. For many years she was a keen ice skater and in 1968 she took part in the National Figure Skating Championship finals.

Vera's early career included being a fashion journalist for *Vogue* magazine for 16 years, followed by a few years as Design Director for Ralph Lauren. However, when she got married in 1989 she realized there was a market for simple yet sexy wedding dresses. In 1990 she launched her own label designing wedding gowns. Her designs brought elegance back to wedding dresses. Since then she has become famous for her evening gowns and ice-skating costumes. Meg Ryan, Sharon Stone and Uma Thurman are all fans of her sophisticated clothes.

In 2003 Vera hit the catwalk with a collection of stunning daywear. As with all her designs she managed to create a feminine look that wasn't too fussy.

Tom Ford

The American designer Tom Ford has been called the most influential designer of recent years. As Creative Director for the Italian label Gucci and the French label Yves Saint Laurent (YSL) he is certainly one of the most important people in the fashion world today.

Tom was born in Texas, USA in 1962. He trained as an actor before studying interior design and fashion in New York and Paris. He was hired by Gucci in 1990 and took charge of business in 1994. It is thanks to Tom that Gucci changed creative direction and created a glamorous new line that included slinky velvet hipster trousers and tight satin skirts. Today, Tom designs Gucci's womenswear and menswear as well as shoes, watches and luggage.

Tom's success in turning Gucci's fortunes around has won him many fashion awards. In 2000 Gucci also acquired the famous French house of YSL. Tom has worked closely with the creative teams at YSL to bring the company back up-to-date and ready to compete in the fashion industry of the twenty-first century.

Miuccia Prada

The Italian leather goods company of Prada has been around since 1913. But it wasn't until 1978, when Miuccia Prada took charge of the family business, that it became one of the most fashionable labels of our time.

Born in 1949, Miuccia is the granddaugher of Mario Prada, the founder of the Prada label. With a PhD in Political Science, Miuccia didn't seem the obvious choice for Director of the family business. However, when Miuccia took control she modernized the old-fashioned company. In 1985 her nylon black handbags were snapped up by supermodels and fashion editors.

The success of the new Prada bags led to her introducing a line of women's wear in 1989. Her simple yet sophisticated designs caught on and in 1992 she launched a new line called Miu Miu. Aimed at younger people these fashions were less expensive and more casual.

Miuccia has taken Prada from strength to strength. In 1995 she launched a menswear collection. Today, she is one of the most powerful women in the fashion industry.

Tommy Hilfiger

Tommy Hilfiger produces casual clothes for streetwise people. His fashions and fragrances are worn by celebrities like Britney Spears and Beyoncé Knowles. The American designer was born in 1951 in the town of Elmira, New York. He was still a teenager when he opened his first shop in New York. 'The People's Place' specialized in hippy clothes, especially bell-bottom jeans. Unfortunately Tommy went bankrupt, but in the 1970s he bounced back and began designing his own clothes.

In 1985 Tommy launched his own label. He produced easy-to-wear clothes he claimed were 'for the people'. For many years his main market was middle-class, white Americans. That all changed in 1990 when the rap star Snoop Doggy Dog wore one of his shirts on television. Suddenly, his label became more trendy and popular with younger people. In 1995 he became Menswear Designer of the Year in America. He now heads of one of the most popular designer labels in the world.

Index